Space

Ben Denne and Eileen O'Brien

Designed by
Cristina Adami and Neil Francis

Additional designs by Catherine Mackinnon

Illustrated by Andy Burton

Series editor: Gillian Doherty
Managing editor: Jane Chisholm
Managing designer: Mary Cartwright
Photographic manipulation: John Russell
Scientific consultant: Stuart Atkinson

Contents

Internet links

Look out for the Internet links boxes throughout this book. They contain descriptions of Web sites where you can find out more about space. For links to these Web sites, go to the **Usborne Quicklinks Web site** at **www.usborne-quicklinks.com** and type the keywords "discovery space".

★ You will also find symbols like this one next to some of the pictures. Wherever you see one of these symbols, it means that you can download the picture from the **Usborne Quicklinks Web site**. For more information on using the Internet, and downloading Usborne pictures, see inside the front cover and page 46.

An astronaut repairing the Hubble Space Telescope

What's in space?

When you look up at the sky on a clear night, it's possible to see around 3,000 stars. But what you see is only a tiny fraction of space. Space is enormous and full of amazing things. Together, everything in space is known as the universe, or cosmos.

The universe

The universe is so huge that no one really knows for sure exactly how big it is. It is made up of billions of stars, planets, moons, enormous clouds of gas and the giant empty spaces in between.

Stars

A star is a massive ball of hot gas that gives off heat and light. Stars are much larger than Earth. Our nearest star, the Sun, is 150 million km (93 million miles) away.

Light years

Distances in space are so vast that they are measured in units called "light years". Light is the fastest thing in the universe. It travels 300,000km (186,000 miles) per second. A light year is the distance light travels in one year, which is 9.46 million million* km (5.88 million million miles).

Galaxies

Galaxies are enormous groups of stars. They can contain millions or even billions of stars and there are millions of galaxies in the universe. Our Sun is part of the Milky Way galaxy, which is 100,000 light years across.

The broad band of stars above the trees is part of the Milky Way galaxy.

* U.S. = trillion

Planets

A planet is a gigantic ball of rock or gas that revolves around, or orbits, a star. Earth is one of nine planets that orbit the Sun. Together, the Sun and everything that orbits it are known as the Solar System.

Here you can see the Sun and planets of our Solar System. (The planets are not shown to scale.)

Moons

Many of the planets in our Solar System have one or more moons. Moons orbit planets in the same way that planets orbit stars. Earth's moon is smaller than Earth and has a very rocky surface.

Odds and ends

There are also smaller objects, called asteroids, comets and meteoroids, that form part of our Solar System. These are chunks of rock, dust, metal or ice and they orbit the Sun like miniature planets.

Internet links

For a link to a Web site where you can play space games and download a spacey screensaver, go to **www.usborne-quicklinks.com**

Fact: Earth's second nearest star, Alpha Centauri C, is 4.21 light years away. It would take a jet plane over four and a half million years to get there.

How the universe began ....

No one really knows for sure how the universe began, but there's a theory that it may have started with an enormous explosion. This is known as the "Big Bang" theory.

The Big Bang

According to the theory, around 15,000 million years ago, a huge explosion took place, which made an incredibly hot fireball. Scientists don't really know what caused it.

The picture on the left shows what the Big Bang might have looked like.

After the Big Bang

Eventually, the fireball began to cool and form really tiny pieces, called particles. These particles became the building blocks of the universe, and everything in the universe now is made up of them. Gradually, the particles spread out and the universe began to expand.

The earliest galaxies

As the fireball cooled even more, it formed thick gases, which then collected into dense pockets. The pockets gradually became more and more dense, until eventually stars formed and the earliest galaxies were born.

Our Solar System

About 10,000 million years after the Big Bang, our Sun formed. Vast clouds of gas swirling around it became the planets and moons of our Solar System. Today, parts of the universe are still forming from dense clumps of gas.

The planets in our Solar System formed from clouds of gas like these.

The Sun

How do we know?

Astronomers are convinced that the Big Bang theory is correct because powerful equipment has detected a faint signal, or echo, in space. They believe this echo is from the Big Bang explosion.

What's next?

The force of the Big Bang was so great that the universe is still expanding. Some scientists think it will expand forever. If it did, everything would fade away and the universe would become a mist of cold particles.

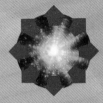

The universe is still expanding after the Big Bang.

Other scientists think that a force called gravity will slow down this expansion, and pull everything back together until all the galaxies collide, creating a Big Crunch.

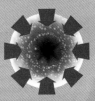

In a Big Crunch, gravity could pull everything together.

Bang, crunch, bang

There's also a theory that the universe expands, then shrinks, then expands again. So, a Big Bang is followed by a Big Crunch, then another Big Bang and so on, in a repeating pattern.

The universe could work like a heart beating, with a Big Crunch after a Big Bang in a repeating cycle.

Big Bang   Big Crunch   Big Bang

Internet links

For a link to a Web site where you can watch a short movie about the Big Bang, go to **www.usborne-quicklinks.com**

Space watch

For thousands of years, people have gazed up at the sky and wondered about the mysteries of the universe. Now, using powerful telescopes, people are able to study the universe in greater detail than ever before. People who study space are called astronomers.

Optical telescopes

These are the Keck telescopes in Hawaii, two of the largest optical telescopes in the world. Each one stands eight stories high.

Optical telescopes create images using light. Images are magnified, or made bigger, by using mirrors or special curved pieces of glass called lenses. Very large, powerful optical telescopes are housed in buildings called observatories.

This group of 27 enormous radio telescopes, in New Mexico in the U.S.A., is called the Very Large Array. The telescopes are used to study galaxies and other parts of our universe.

Radio telescopes

Radio telescopes enable astronomers to see objects deep in space, which can't be seen using optical telescopes. This type of telescope uses a dish or antenna to collect signals, called radio waves, that are given off by objects in space. Information from radio telescopes is fed into computers which turn it into pictures.

Space telescopes

In the 20th century, scientists discovered how to send telescopes into space. Telescopes in space can be used to see much farther and more clearly than telescopes on Earth, because the Earth's atmosphere (see page 20) doesn't block their view.

These solar panels attached to Hubble collect energy from the Sun.

The Hubble Space Telescope

The first major space telescope was the Hubble Space Telescope, or HST, an optical telescope launched in 1990. Hubble orbits the Earth at a distance of around 612km (380 miles) and is about the size of a bus. Astronomers on Earth send instructions to cameras on board to take pictures of distant galaxies and planets. The HST makes its own power by collecting energy from the Sun.

Glasses for Hubble

Soon after Hubble was launched, astronomers noticed that it was sending back blurred images. They realized that there was a fault in the telescope.

So, in 1993, a team was sent to Hubble to fix it. They attached new equipment that worked like glasses. Ever since, Hubble has sent back amazing pictures of the universe.

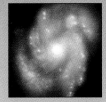

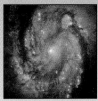

Pictures taken before (top) and after (bottom) Hubble was repaired

Fact: Each day, the Hubble Space Telescope collects enough information to fill five encyclopedias.

Our Solar System ....

Solar means "of the Sun". Our Solar System is the Sun and everything that orbits it. It's not the only solar system in the Milky Way galaxy, however. Recently, astronomers have begun to discover other planets orbiting stars far out in space.

This picture shows the Sun and the planets of our Solar System in orbit around it. (They are not shown to scale.)

The outer and inner planets are separated by a band of asteroids called the Asteroid Belt.

The Sun

Like all stars, the Sun is an enormous ball of exploding gas. It applies a pulling force, known as gravity, to everything within a range of around 6,000 million km (4,000 million miles). Gravity locks all the planets in orbit around the Sun.

Mars

The Sun

Venus

Earth

Mercury

The planets

So far, scientists know of nine planets in our Solar System, but there may be others yet to be discovered. The planets all travel in near-circular orbits around the Sun, spinning as they do so.

The four planets nearest the Sun are Mercury, Venus, Earth and Mars. These planets have rocky surfaces and are known as the inner planets. The outer planets – Jupiter, Saturn, Uranus, Neptune and Pluto – are made mostly of gas, ice and liquid.

Beyond Pluto, there's a band of icy rocks named the Kuiper Belt. Even farther away is a band of comets, called the Oort Cloud.

Pluto

The farther a planet is from the Sun, the colder it is.

Saturn

Neptune

Uranus

Jupiter

Days and years

A planet's day is the time it takes for it to spin around once. An Earth day, for example, lasts 24 hours, but a day on Jupiter only lasts ten hours. A planet's year is the length of time it takes to orbit the Sun once. Earth's year is 365.26 days long and a year on Venus is 225 days long.

Gravity

On Earth, if you throw a ball in the air it comes down again. What pulls the ball back is something called gravity. Without gravity, the ball would go up into space. There is gravity on all the other planets and moons too. How strong the pull is depends on how big and heavy the planet is. On planets bigger and heavier than Earth, the pull is stronger, making objects feel heavier than on Earth. On smaller and lighter planets, the pull is weaker, so objects feel lighter.

Internet links

For a link to a Web site where you can watch a short movie about gravity or take a quiz, go to **www.usborne-quicklinks.com**

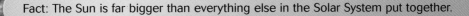

Fact: The Sun is far bigger than everything else in the Solar System put together.

The Sun ....

The Sun is the most important thing in our Solar System. It gives the planets their heat and light, and its gravity stops them from flying off into space. Life on Earth wouldn't exist without the Sun.

Great ball of fire

The Sun is a huge ball of burning gases. It is a relatively small star, measuring around 1.4 million km (870,000 miles) across. The Sun has been burning for over 4,000 million years and will probably continue to burn for around another 5,000 million years, until it burns out and dies (see page 33).

The dark areas on this picture of the Sun are called sunspots.

This is a cutaway diagram to show the structure of the Sun.

The middle of the Sun is the hottest part. Temperatures can reach 15 million°C (59 million°F).

The Sun's surface is made of churning gases.

This part carries the heat produced in the middle of the Sun up to the surface.

Sunspots

Dark patches called sunspots sometimes appear on the Sun's surface. These are areas that are cooler than their surroundings. Sunspots are usually quite small but sometimes lots of them join together to cover an enormous area. The largest area yet seen covered in sunspots was over 18,000 million square km (7,000 million square miles).

Internet links

For a link to a Web site where you can browse hundreds of pictures and movies of the Sun taken by the SOHO spacecraft, go to **www.usborne-quicklinks.com**

Fact: If you could stand on the Sun, you probably wouldn't be able to move. The Sun's strong gravity would make you around twenty-eight times heavier.

Fiery flares

Sometimes, when energy builds up in an area on the outer layer of the Sun, it flares up, heating gases to millions of degrees and blasting jets of burning gas into space. These violent explosions look like flames and are known as solar flares and prominences.

This picture, showing solar flares rising out of the Sun, was taken by a spacecraft called SOHO, which is used to take pictures of the Sun.

Here you can see the solar wind lighting up the sky in beautiful greens and blues in Manitoba, in Canada.

Light shows

The Sun blows a constant, invisible stream of gas out into space. This is called solar wind. When wind gets trapped near Earth's North or South Poles, it reacts with the air on Earth and makes a beautiful light display, called an *aurora*. In the north, this is called the *aurora borealis*, or the northern lights. In the south, it is called the *aurora australis*, or the southern lights.

Planet probing

Most space exploration doesn't involve sending people into space. Instead, spacecraft are sent. They can work in the harsh conditions of distant planets, where humans wouldn't survive.

Satellites

Any object that orbits another object is called a satellite. Moons orbiting planets are natural satellites. Artificial satellites are machines that orbit a planet or moon and gather information about it.

What do satellites do?

Earth's artificial satellites have many different uses. Some gather information about the weather. Others pick up radio, TV or telephone signals from one place and send them back down to other places on Earth.

An artificial satellite

What is NASA?

The Vehicle Assembly Building at NASA's John F. Kennedy Space Center in the U.S.A. It is from this Space Center that the Space Shuttle (see page 17) is launched.

NASA, the National Aeronautics and Space Administration, organizes space exploration on behalf of the U.S. government. NASA leads the world in space exploration. Other space organizations include the European Space Agency and the Russian Space Agency.

> ### Internet links
> For a link to a Web site with the latest information on current space probe missions, go to
> **www.usborne-quicklinks.com**

Space probes

Spacecraft called probes are also sent to explore space. Probes carry special equipment, including cameras to take pictures of distant planets. All the planets in our Solar System, except Pluto, have been visited by probes. Some just fly close to planets, others orbit them and some carry smaller probes that are dropped onto planets.

The picture on the left is the space probe Magellan just before it was released from the Space Shuttle *Atlantis*. Magellan was sent to study Venus in 1991. The planet in the background is Earth.

A journey to Jupiter

In 1989, a spacecraft called Galileo was sent to study Jupiter. It arrived at its destination six years later and has been orbiting the planet ever since.

The Galileo spacecraft was launched into space inside the Space Shuttle *Atlantis* (see page 17).

As soon as it had left Earth, Galileo broke away from *Atlantis* and continued its journey to Jupiter alone.

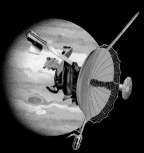

In 1995, Galileo reached Jupiter and began orbiting the planet. It sent back lots of information.

Five months after it arrived, Galileo dropped a smaller probe onto the planet itself.

Fact: The space probe Voyager 1 is currently the farthest man-made object from Earth. It is over 12 thousand million km (7.5 thousand million miles) away.

Journey to space

For hundreds of years, people dreamed of going to space. But space travel only became possible when, in the 1950s, scientists developed a rocket powerful enough for the journey. Since then, more than 100 people have journeyed to space.

The race to space

In the 1950s and 1960s, the U.S.A. and the U.S.S.R. (now Russia) competed to be the first country to send a rocket into space. The Soviets achieved this in 1957. In 1961, they became the first to send a human, Yuri Gagarin.

Yuri Gagarin, just before his historic journey to space

Men on the Moon

In 1968, an American mission, Apollo 8, sent the first manned spacecraft to fly around the Moon. Then, in 1969, three astronauts went to the Moon as part of the Apollo 11 mission. One of the crew, Neil Armstrong, became the first man to walk on its surface.

Unlucky 13

In 1970, three American astronauts set off for the Moon as part of the Apollo 13 mission. Two days after take-off, an explosion left their spacecraft without power. The astronauts managed to bring it back to Earth four days later, but they almost ran out of air on the way.

Internet links

For a link to a Web site where you can see pictures and watch movies of the Space Shuttle, go to www.usborne-quicklinks.com

Astronaut Neil Armstrong preparing to put on his helmet just before his trip to the Moon in 1969

The Space Shuttle *Columbia* taking off from the Kennedy Space Center in Florida in the U.S.A.

The Space Shuttle

Until 1981, when the Space Shuttle made its first journey to space, spacecraft could only be used once. The Space Shuttle became the first spacecraft that could be used again and again. NASA has a fleet of shuttles called *Columbia*, *Discovery*, *Atlantis* and *Endeavour*. They are used to carry people, satellites and equipment to space. They can take off vertically like rockets and land horizontally like aircraft.

In the future

Scientists have come up with lots of new and exciting ideas for space travel. But space travel is very expensive, so engineers are trying to develop spacecraft that are cheaper to run.

One idea that engineers have had is for a series of spacecraft called Reusable Launch Vehicles, or RLVs. Like the Space Shuttle, RLVs could be used again and again, but they would be cheaper to run.

This is an illustration of a proposed NASA Reusable Launch Vehicle called the Space Express Rocket.

Fact: The first creature to travel in space was not a human; it was a Russian dog named Laika, in 1957.

Living in space

A space station is a large spacecraft used to carry out experiments, or as a base for space exploration. Astronauts often stay on board for long periods. They need to be able to eat, sleep and exercise in an environment with almost no gravity.

This photograph shows astronauts floating inside a space station.

Floating lifestyle

Gravity is made by large objects and planets, such as Earth. In space there is hardly any gravity. Everything must be adapted to work without it.

This astronaut is working on an experiment in a space station. Her feet are placed in straps attached to the floor to stop her from floating away.

Since there's no gravity, astronauts can sleep comfortably standing up, or even upside down.

This is a toilet on the Space Shuttle. Space toilets use a machine a bit like a vacuum cleaner to suck waste away.

Keeping cool

Space temperatures are too extreme for people to bear. The temperature just outside the Earth's atmosphere, for example, rises to 121°C (250°F) in sunlight, but can drop to -121°C (-185°F) in the shade. Spacecraft are made from special materials, to keep the temperature inside at a comfortable level for humans.

Space food

Because there is very little gravity in space, food won't stay on a plate. To overcome this problem, astronaut meals used to come in the form of a paste, stored in a special tube.

Today, space food is far tastier. Meals for space missions are dried and sealed in packets. They are then mixed with water just before they are eaten. Wet food sticks together, making it easy to eat in a low-gravity environment.

This picture shows some space food. All the food has to be sealed until it is eaten, to stop it from floating around.

Fact: The longest time ever spent constantly in space was more than a year. Vladimir Polyakov spent 1 year and 72 days on the Mir Space Station.

Earth and the Moon

Earth is the third planet from the Sun, and the only planet in the Solar System where we know life exists. It has only one moon, which is about a quarter of the Earth's size. This is unusually large for a moon. Most moons are tiny compared to the planets that they orbit.

Earth file
- Average distance from Sun: 150 million km (93 million miles)
- Diameter: 12,756km (7,927 miles)
- Time to orbit Sun: 365.26 Earth days
- Rotation time: 23hrs, 56mins
- Number of satellites: 1

Living planet

Earth has excellent conditions for life. Its distance from the Sun gives it the perfect temperature range. Earth also has air and water on it. If these were missing, life could never exist here.

Conditions on Earth are just right for life to exist. The picture on the left shows some of the 30 million different types of life on Earth.

Protecting the planet

The atmosphere of a planet is the layer of gases that surrounds it. Earth's atmosphere works like a shield around the planet, filtering out harmful rays from the Sun. It also traps some of the Sun's heat against the planet's surface, helping to keep the temperature steady.

This diagram shows the thickness of the atmosphere (in red) around Earth.

Moon shapes

The Moon looks bright because it reflects the Sun's light. It doesn't give out any light of its own. As it orbits Earth, the amount of the sunlit side we can see varies. This makes it look as if the Moon changes shape every day.

The Moon's different shapes are called phases. Here are some of them:

New moon   Crescent

Half moon   Full moon

Pulling the oceans

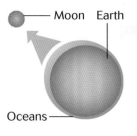

Moon   Earth

Oceans

This diagram shows the Moon's gravity pulling the oceans.

The Moon is held in orbit by Earth's gravity, but the pull of the Moon's gravity also affects the Earth. As the Moon orbits Earth, its pull makes the sea level in the oceans rise and fall. The changing sea level is called the tide.

Moon missions

People have been to the Moon several times. The first people to land there were the crew members of the Apollo 11 mission, in 1969. In 1998, a NASA craft found evidence of ice at the Moon's poles. If there is water on the Moon, it might be possible to set up a permanent base there.

Internet links

For a link to a Web site where you'll find amazing pictures of Earth taken from space, go to **www.usborne-quicklinks.com**

Astronaut Buzz Aldrin walking on the Moon in 1969

Fact: The Moon spins at the same speed as Earth, so the same side of it is always facing us. The other side is called the "dark side of the Moon".

Mercury ....

Mercury is the closest planet to the Sun. It is a barren, rocky planet that looks a lot like Earth's moon. The surface of Mercury is covered with huge holes, or craters, where rocks called meteorites have crashed into it.

Mercury file
- Average distance from Sun: 58 million km (36 million miles)
- Diameter: 4,880km (3,032 miles)
- Time to orbit Sun: 88 Earth days
- Rotation time: 59 Earth days
- Number of satellites: 0

Here you can see the crater-covered surface of Mercury, with the Sun behind it.

Hot and cold

Mercury gets hot because it is so close to the Sun, but it can get very cold as well. The planet spins around very slowly. This means that parts of it are exposed to the Sun's heat for long periods of time, then cut off from the Sun for equally long periods.

Meteor madness

The largest crater on Mercury is the Caloris Basin. On the opposite side of the planet is a mountainous area known as the Weird Terrain. Scientists think that the meteorite that made the Caloris Basin created the Weird Terrain as well. Here's what they think happened:

Thousands of years ago, a huge meteorite struck Mercury.

Shock waves passed through Mercury, creating the Weird Terrain.

Weird Terrain

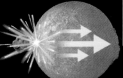

Meteorite

Shock waves

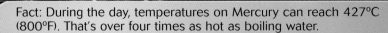

Fact: During the day, temperatures on Mercury can reach 427°C (800°F). That's over four times as hot as boiling water.

Venus

Venus is about the same size as Earth, and the closest planet to it. Venus is an easy planet to spot from Earth. After the Sun and Earth's moon, it's the brightest thing in the sky.

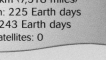

Venus file
- Average distance from Sun: 108 million km (67 million miles)
- Diameter: 12,100km (7,518 miles)
- Time to orbit Sun: 225 Earth days
- Rotation time: 243 Earth days
- Number of satellites: 0

Burning rain

Venus's rain could dissolve a human being. The clouds it comes from are made from a strong acid called sulphuric acid. This rain would burn the surface of Venus, but the atmosphere is so hot that it turns the rain into mist long before it reaches the planet's surface.

Volcanic planet

Venus has lots of volcanoes. In the past they erupted, throwing out extremely hot molten (melted) rock, called lava. The lava flowed over the surrounding area and then hardened. Most of Venus's surface is coated in hard lava.

This is a photograph of a volcano called Gula Mons on Venus's surface.

Heat trap

Venus is the hottest planet in the Solar System. It is surrounded by a thick layer of clouds. Any heat from the Sun that finds its way into the atmosphere gets trapped between the clouds and the planet's surface. The surface temperature of Venus can get as high as 480°C (896°F).

Here you can see how Venus's atmosphere traps heat against its surface.

Rays from the Sun pass into Venus's atmosphere.

Venus's thick clouds stop the Sun's rays from escaping.

Trapped heat

Fact: Venus takes more time to spin around once than it does to orbit the Sun. This means that Venus's day is longer than its year.

Mars ....

Mars is the fourth planet from the Sun. Scientists think that there may once have been life there, and are researching this theory. Lots of missions to Mars are going on now, and many more are planned for the future.

Mars file
- Average distance from Sun: 228 million km (142 million miles)
- Diameter: 6,786km (4,217 miles)
- Time to orbit Sun: 687 Earth days
- Rotation time: 24hrs, 37mins
- Number of satellites: 2

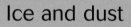

Ice and dust

Mars is cold and dusty. Its soil contains lots of iron, which makes the planet appear rusty red. All the water on Mars's surface is frozen into ice. However, there is evidence that there could have been flowing water there in the past. If there was once water on Mars, then living things may have existed there.

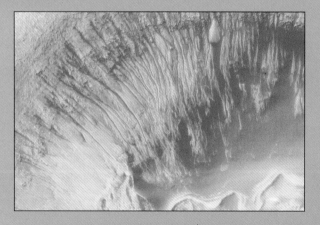

Channels like these are strong evidence that Mars once had flowing water on its surface.

Dust storms

The climate on Mars is cold and harsh. Temperatures can drop to as low as -123°C (-190°F). Fierce storms sometimes blast across the planet's surface, stirring the dust up into huge clouds. These storms can cover the whole planet.

Meteorite from Mars

In 1996, scientists analysed a meteorite that had come from Mars. Some of them claimed that the meteorite contained ancient remains of tiny creatures. If this is true, then it proves that life once existed on Mars.

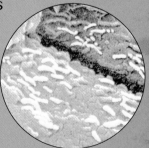

This picture shows part of the Mars meteorite, seen through a microscope. The bits shown in yellow could be the remains of ancient creatures.

Fact: The largest volcano in the Solar System is on Mars. It is over 27km (17 miles) tall. That's over three times higher than the tallest volcano on Earth.

This photograph of Mars was taken by a probe called the Viking probe.

Exploring the surface

In July 1997, NASA's Pathfinder spacecraft landed on Mars. Inside was a vehicle called the Sojourner, which was operated by NASA scientists on Earth. It drove around taking photographs of the planet's surface.

Mars and Earth

Billions of years ago, conditions on Mars and Earth may have been very similar. Scientists think that studying Mars might help us learn about Earth's future.

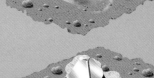

A covering of balloons protected the Pathfinder spacecraft as it crashed onto Mars's surface.

Once Pathfinder had landed safely, the balloons deflated and fell away.

Pathfinder opened up on the surface of Mars, to let Sojourner out.

Internet links

For a link to a Web site where you can find out more about a planned mission to Mars, go to **www.usborne-quicklinks.com**

★

This photograph of the Sojourner vehicle was taken by Pathfinder on Mars, and beamed back to Earth.

Jupiter

Jupiter is the largest planet in our Solar System. It is so large that if it was hollow all the other planets would fit inside it.

Jupiter file
- Average distance from Sun: 778 million km (483 million miles)
- Diameter: 142,984km (88,850 miles)
- Time to orbit Sun: 11.9 Earth years
- Rotation time: 9hrs, 50mins
- Number of satellites: 29

King of the gas giants

Four of the planets in our Solar System – Jupiter, Saturn, Uranus and Neptune – are made mostly of gas. They are known as the gas giants. The only solid part of Jupiter is its core, which is made of rock.

Jupiter's moons

Jupiter has 29 moons that we know of, and new ones are still being found. The four largest were discovered 400 years ago by an astronomer named Galileo. They are called the Galilean moons.

Io is covered in volcanoes. One, called Pilan Patera, has eruptions up to 139km (86 miles) high.

Europa is completely covered in ice. It is the smoothest object in the Solar System.

Ganymede is the largest moon in the Solar System. It is even larger than the planet Mercury.

Callisto is made mostly of ice. The largest known crater in the Solar System, Valhalla, is on Callisto.

Jupiter looks solid, even though it is made mostly of gas. You can see its four largest moons on the right.

Solid gas

At the surface of Jupiter, the gas is about the same thickness as the gas in Earth's atmosphere. Nearer Jupiter's core, the gas gets hotter and thicker, becoming more like soupy liquid than gas. Next to the core, Jupiter's gas is so thick that it is almost solid.

Fact: The Great Red Spot is a huge storm raging on Jupiter's surface. It covers an area 14,000km (8,700 miles) wide.

Saturn ....

Saturn is smaller than Jupiter, but it is still huge. Like Jupiter, it is mainly made up of dense gas. Saturn is famous for the enormous rings around it. All the gas giants have these rings, but Saturn's are brighter and bigger than all the others.

Saturn file
- Average distance from Sun: 1,427 million km (887 million miles)
- Diameter: 120,536km (74,901 miles)
- Time to orbit Sun: 29.5 Earth years
- Rotation time: 10hrs, 14mins
- Number of satellites: 30

Saturn's rings

Saturn's rings are actually icy boulders and rocks orbiting the planet. They range from dust particles to chunks the size of a car. Saturn's rings are over 300,000km (186,000 miles) in diameter, but only about 1km (0.6 miles) thick.

Life on Titan

Titan is one of Saturn's moons. It has a thick atmosphere, which shields it from the harsh conditions of space. Scientists think that there may be life on Titan.

This is a photograph of Titan. Its atmosphere may make it possible for life to exist there.

Saturn's rings can easily be seen from Earth using a telescope.

Fact: Although Saturn is huge, it is so light that if you could find a swimming pool big enough to drop it in, it would float.

The distant planets

The farthest planets from the Sun are Uranus, Neptune and Pluto. Studying these planets is difficult, because they are so far away.

Uranus

Uranus is the seventh planet from the Sun. It is over 19 times farther from the Sun than Earth is. Uranus has 21 moons that we know of, including one that hasn't been named yet.

Strange spinner

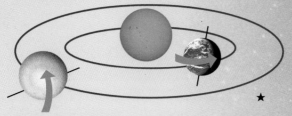

This diagram shows Uranus's spin, compared to the spin of the Earth.

Uranus spins at a different angle from all the other planets. Some scientists think that this strange spin was caused by a collision with something in the past that knocked Uranus onto its side.

Uranus's rings

Uranus has rings around it, like the other gas giants. The rings are made of dust, so a powerful telescope is needed to see them. They were discovered in 1977.

This planet is Uranus. The planet on the right is Neptune.

You can clearly see Uranus's dust rings in the picture above.

Uranus file
- Average distance from Sun: 2,871 million km (1,784 million miles)
- Diameter: 51,118km (31,765 miles)
- Time to orbit Sun: 84 Earth years
- Rotation time: 17hrs, 54mins
- Number of satellites: 21

Internet links

For a link to a Web site where you'll discover more about the distant planets, go to
www.usborne-quicklinks.com

Fact: Uranus is the farthest planet from the Sun that can be seen with the naked eye. You need a telescope to see the two planets beyond it.

Neptune

Neptune is the smallest of the gas giants, but it is still over 17 times the size of Earth. Neptune has a violent atmosphere and the fastest winds in the Solar System. The winds travel at speeds of up to 2,000kph (1,240mph).

The Great Dark Spot, above, is a dark area which sometimes appears on Neptune. Scientists think it may be a storm the size of Earth.

Blue and green planets

Uranus and Neptune both have a gas called methane in their atmospheres. Methane absorbs red light and reflects blue light, so these planets look blue and green from space.

Neptune file
- Average distance from Sun: 4,500 million km (2,800 million miles)
- Diameter: 49,528km (30,775 miles)
- Time to orbit Sun: 165 Earth years
- Rotation time: 19hrs, 12mins
- Number of satellites: 8

Pluto

Pluto is a tiny planet made from rock and ice. It is usually the farthest planet from the Sun. However, it has a very strange orbit. For 20 years of its 248-year orbit, it is closer to the Sun than Neptune is.

Pluto file
- Average distance from Sun: 5,913 million km (3,674 million miles)
- Diameter: 2,400km (1,491 miles)
- Time to orbit Sun: 248 Earth years
- Rotation time: 6 Earth days, 10hrs
- Number of satellites: 1

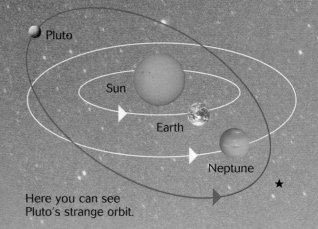

Pluto

Sun

Earth

Neptune

Here you can see Pluto's strange orbit.

Fact: Some astronomers don't think that Pluto should be classed as a planet. They argue that it is too small.

Asteroids and comets

The Sun and planets are the largest objects in the Solar System, but there are lots of smaller ones. They are called asteroids, meteoroids and comets.

Asteroids and meteoroids

Asteroids are big lumps of rock or metal that travel through space. Meteoroids are tiny space rocks. There are millions of asteroids and meteoroids in our Solar System. Most of them are concentrated into a huge ring between Mars and Jupiter, called the Asteroid Belt.

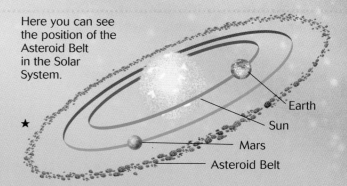

Here you can see the position of the Asteroid Belt in the Solar System.

Earth
Sun
Mars
Asteroid Belt

Meteorites

Meteoroids sometimes fly so close to the Earth that they are sucked in by its gravity. Meteoroids that enter the Earth's atmosphere are called meteors. Meteors that survive to reach the ground are called meteorites. Large meteorites can do quite a lot of damage.

This picture shows what asteroids might look like.

A comet shooting
through space

Shooting stars and meteors

As meteors enter the atmosphere a lot
of heat is created, so small meteors
burn up before they reach the Earth's
surface. As they burn up, they glow
brightly. These meteors are called
shooting stars.

Meteors create white streaks
across the sky as they
burn up.

This shows what
happens when
meteors enter
the Earth's
atmosphere.

★

Comets

Comets are huge lumps of dirty ice,
mixed with dust and grit. Most of them
have enormous, oval-shaped orbits. This
means that they only come near the Sun
for short periods of time. During these
periods, comets are described as active.

Melting comets

When a comet becomes
active, the Sun's rays heat it up
and it starts to melt. As it melts, it
releases gases and dust trapped in its
ice. They stream out behind the comet,
creating a tail which can be up to 320
million km (200 million miles) long.

Mass extinction

A meteorite hitting the Earth might make a
crater, but an asteroid or comet could
cause more damage than a thousand
nuclear bombs. Asteroids and comets
have crashed into the Earth before, with
catastrophic results. Some scientists think
it was an asteroid that killed the dinosaurs.

Fact: If all the asteroids in the Solar System were weighed together, their
weight would still be less than the weight of the smallest planet, Pluto.

The life of a star

Stars are huge balls of exploding gas which burn for billions of years. The appearance of stars varies according to their temperature: very hot stars are blue, medium ones are yellow, and older, cooler stars are red.

Protostars

Stars begin their lives in huge clouds called nebulas, made up of tiny pieces, or particles, of gas and dust. Over thousands of years, these particles are drawn together by gravity. They form smaller, shrinking clouds. These clouds are called protostars.

This is a photograph of the Horsehead Nebula, taken by the Hubble telescope.

Creating light

As a protostar shrinks, the particles begin to collide and rub against each other, creating heat and light. Eventually the protostar becomes so hot that the particles in it begin to fuse, or join together, creating a huge amount of energy which explodes outward.

Gravity pulls the particles in a protostar together. The middle of the protostar gets more and more concentrated.

As particles in the protostar rub together, heat and light are created. The protostar begins to glow.

The particles in the protostar fuse together and then explode outward as heat and light. A star has been born.

Internet links

For a link to a Web site where you can see lots of amazing pictures of stars, go to **www.usborne-quicklinks.com**

Length of life

A star starts to die when its supply of gas runs out. Small stars just fade away. Bigger stars grow even bigger and cooler, changing from yellow or blue to red. At this stage, a star is known as a red giant.

When a big star dies, it may blow up in a huge explosion called a supernova. This is a photograph of one.

Small but heavy

Eventually, a red giant pushes its outer layers into space. All that is left is a tiny star known as a white dwarf. White dwarf stars are very dense and heavy for their size. Their weight gives them an enormous amount of gravity.

Black holes

Sometimes, when a big star dies, it collapses and creates a black hole. Black holes are like giant vacuum cleaners in space. They are so dense and heavy that their gravity sucks in everything around them. Black holes even suck in light instead of reflecting it, which makes them invisible.

Everything is sucked into a black hole in a giant spiral.

The bright dot near the middle of this picture is a white dwarf star. It is surrounded by clouds of gas.

This shows what a black hole might look like if it were visible.

Fact: A piece of a white dwarf the size of a marble could weigh up to 900 tonnes (885 tons).

Galaxies

Stars aren't randomly scattered throughout the universe. They form groups which are known as galaxies. Our Sun, Earth and the rest of our Solar System make up a tiny part of the Milky Way galaxy.

Galaxy shapes

Galaxies are different shapes and sizes. After the Big Bang, gravity caused the first stars to group together to form different types. The two most common galaxy shapes are spiral and elliptical.

This is a spiral galaxy. This type of galaxy has a central bar or bulge with two or more curved arms.

Elliptical galaxies, like the one in this picture, vary in shape from round to oval. They usually contain lots of old stars.

In spiral galaxies, like the one in the photograph on the left, young stars are usually found in the arms, and older stars are found in the central bulge.

Doing cartwheels

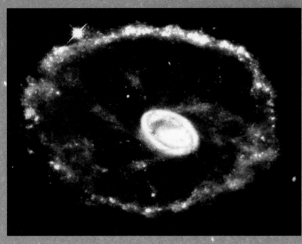

The Cartwheel galaxy is an irregular galaxy.

As well as spiral and elliptical galaxies, there are also irregular galaxies. These form many different shapes. Some are just clouds of stars without a definite shape. A galaxy often becomes irregular when it collides with another galaxy. The Cartwheel galaxy's shape was created when a smaller galaxy crashed into it, around 200 million years ago.

Groups of galaxies

Galaxies are also in groups. The Milky Way forms part of a group called the Local Group. This is a fairly small group, with only around 30 galaxies. Some groups contain as many as 2,500 galaxies.

The Milky Way

Most astronomers think the Milky Way galaxy is spiral-shaped. Compared with other galaxies, the Milky Way is fairly large, measuring around 100,000 light years across. Our Solar System lies about 28,000 light years from the middle of the Milky Way.

Seeing the Milky Way

On a clear night, you may be able to see a broad band of stars stretching across the sky. This is part of the Milky Way galaxy. In ancient times, people thought this looked like a trail of spilled milk, which is how our galaxy got its name.

Viewed from the side, the Milky Way has a bulge in the middle.

Our Solar System is located about here in the Milky Way.

Internet links

For a link to a Web site where you can explore the universe and take a virtual tour of the Milky Way and other galaxies, go to **www.usborne-quicklinks.com**

Stargazing

Over thousands of years, people have noticed patterns of bright stars in the night sky. These are called constellations and they are very useful for finding and identifying stars.

These are the stars that make up the constellation Orion. The yellow outline shows the picture it is supposed to represent.

Famous constellations

There are 88 constellations. Many are named after characters from ancient Greek stories. The picture on the right shows the stars in the constellation Orion, a great hunter from these stories. The best way to find constellations is by using a star map. These are maps of the night sky showing the constellations.

This is an example of a star map, showing some of the constellations.

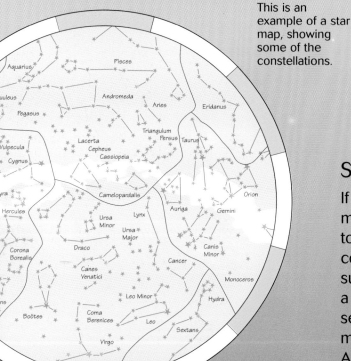

Sky watching

If you want to observe the night sky, make sure you are prepared. You'll need to wear warm clothes, because you'll get cold when sitting or standing still, even in summer. Take binoculars or a telescope, a notepad and pencil to record what you see, and a flashlight for looking at star maps. Never go out in the dark alone. Always go with a parent or guardian, or people from your local astronomy club.

Internet links

For a link to a Web site where you can learn about the night sky and view a different star map for each month, go to www.usborne-quicklinks.com

Telescopes

Telescopes are more powerful than binoculars, but they are more difficult to use and also more expensive. Many of the cheaper ones are not very good. For the cost of a cheap telescope, it's better to buy a good pair of binoculars.

A telescope needs a mount, like the one attached to the telescope in this picture. Without one, you won't be able to hold it steady enough to see anything.

Starry nights

The best time to observe the sky is on a dark, clear night, around two hours after sunset. It's difficult to see much in cities with the glare of city lights, but you will have a better chance if you go to a park. You'll see a lot more in the countryside. Don't give up if you can't see much at first. Your eyes will take up to 20 minutes to adjust to the dark, so you'll see more after a while.

Binoculars

You can see most of the sights in this book with your naked eye, but you'll see much more with a pair of binoculars. Try out several pairs before you buy. A pair of 7x50 binoculars is ideal for looking at stars. It's best not to buy a pair more powerful than 10x50 or they will be too heavy.

Sky events ....

As well as stars and planets, there are lots of other things to see from Earth. Eclipses, meteor showers and comets are just some of the spectacular sky events visible from Earth.

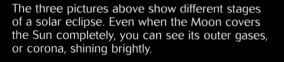

The three pictures above show different stages of a solar eclipse. Even when the Moon covers the Sun completely, you can see its outer gases, or corona, shining brightly.

Seeing a solar eclipse

Never look straight at an eclipse or view it through sunglasses, binoculars or a telescope. The Sun's rays may blind you. However, there are special solar filters that you can watch it through. One of the safest ways to watch a solar eclipse, though, is on TV or on the Internet.

Solar eclipses

A solar eclipse happens when the Moon passes in front of the Sun, cutting off the light to part of Earth. The Moon can cover the Sun because, although it is smaller, it is closer to us. When the Moon covers the whole Sun, this is called a total eclipse. When it covers part of the Sun, it is a partial eclipse.

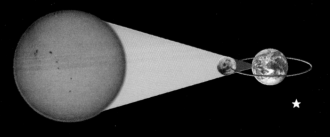

During a solar eclipse, the Moon blocks out the Sun's light, so part of the Earth is in the Moon's shadow.

Fact: In 585BC, a solar eclipse stopped a war in Asia. Both sides were so frightened when they saw it that they immediately stopped fighting.

Shooting stars

On a clear night, you can usually see a few meteors, or shooting stars. But when Earth passes through a stream of dust left by a comet, there are spectacular meteor showers. These occur about once a month in different parts of the world.

Satellite spotting

You can see large satellites and the International Space Station (see page 42) in the night sky with your naked eye. They look like fast-moving points of white light. Be careful not to mistake aircraft for satellites. Aircraft have red and blue identification lights. Keep an eye on astronomy magazines, or the Internet, for information on the position of the International Space Station.

Lunar eclipses

A lunar eclipse happens when the Earth passes between the Sun and the Moon, so that the Moon moves into the Earth's shadow. During a lunar eclipse, the Moon looks dim and it often glows a coppery-brown shade. There is a lunar eclipse most years.

Internet links

For a link to a Web site where there is a fantastic online guide to the night sky, with monthly details of sky events and satellites to watch out for, go to **www.usborne-quicklinks.com**

In a total lunar eclipse, the Moon is in the Earth's shadow.

During a lunar eclipse, the Moon looks coppery-brown. It's perfectly safe to look at with your naked eye, or through binoculars.

The search for life

Is there life beyond planet Earth? We still don't have a definite answer to this question. In the past twenty years, though, scientists have found evidence that there may be life on other planets.

Internet links
For a link to a Web site where you can join the hunt for alien life in space, go to
www.usborne-quicklinks.com

Life on Earth

On Earth, life can be found in the most extreme places. Scientists have found signs of life in fiery volcanoes, at the bottom of the deepest oceans and even inside freezing Arctic ice. If living things can adapt to these harsh conditions, they could probably survive in space.

This is an amphipod, a tiny animal found on Earth at the bottom of very deep oceans.

Where to look?

The Solar System is huge. Before scientists can look for life, they need to know the best places to start looking. There are two essential things a place must have to support life: a source of energy and liquid water. All the planets and moons in the Solar SSystem get energy from the Sun, but only some have water. These are the places where life is most likely to exist.

Covered by clouds

Saturn's moon Titan has a cloudy atmosphere. Scientists think that dark patches under the clouds may be liquid on Titan's surface. A NASA craft called Cassini set off for Saturn in 1997, with a smaller probe called Huygens on board. The Huygens probe will parachute down to Titan's surface and analyze the atmosphere, to see if living things could survive there.

The pictures on the right shows what will happen as the Huygens probe parachutes down to Titan.

270km (168 miles) Probe enters Titan's atmosphere, protected by shield.

180km (112 miles) Probe's parachute opens.

165km (103 miles) Protective front shield and main parachute are discarded.

46km (28.5 miles) Probe passes through Titan's cloud layer.

Probe lands on Titan's surface.

★

Moles on Mars

The European Space Agency hopes to send a craft to Mars in the near future, to search for life. It will take a special device called a mole, which will burrow into the planet's surface and extract a sample of rock to analyze.

Life beneath the ice?

Jupiter's moon Europa has an icy surface. Scientists think there may be oceans of water under the ice that could contain life. NASA hopes to send a mission to Europa to test the thickness of the ice. If they find water, they plan to send a craft to drill through the ice to find out what lies beneath.

Europa's icy surface is too thick to see through, but scientists think that there may be oceans of water under it. This picture shows what the structure of Europa might look like.

Ice on the surface of Europa

Oceans under the ice

The picture on the right is a close-up of the icy surface of Europa.

Man's future in space

Space exploration is becoming more advanced every day, but what does the future hold? Exploring space is expensive, so the answer to this question depends partly on how much money people are willing to spend.

International Space Station

Scientists from 16 countries are building a research station in Earth's orbit. The ISS (International Space Station) will be used to study space and to see how living there affects humans. People are already living on it.

This drawing shows what the ISS will look like when it's finished.

The ISS will be about the size of two soccer fields.

Tourists in orbit

Space tourism could become popular in future, but it would be expensive. The first ever space tourist visited the International Space Station in May 2001. His vacation lasted a week and cost him $20 million.

The first space tourist, Dennis Tito, just after his trip to space

Men on Mars

The technology is available to send people to Mars in the next 20 years, but it would be a difficult task. It would take astronauts about a year to reach Mars. If people make a successful trip to Mars, it might be possible to set up a permanent base there in the future.

This picture shows how a base on Mars might look. Astronauts could use the buggy to explore the planet's surface.

Mining in space

Fuels that are used to make energy will one day run out on Earth. But there may be enormous quantities of them in space, on asteroids, comets and other planets. If we can find ways to obtain them in space, it could solve many of our future energy problems.

Fact: Astronauts on a trip to Mars could be away from Earth for as long as three years.

Glossary

This glossary explains the meaning of important words to do with space. Words in *italic* type have their own entry elsewhere in the glossary.

asteroid A lump of rock or metal orbiting the Sun. Thousands of them are concentrated in a huge ring between Mars and Jupiter, called the Asteroid Belt.

astronaut A person who travels to space, usually after special training. In 2001, however, the first space tourist, Dennis Tito, spent a week on the International Space Station.

astronomer A person who studies space.

atmosphere The layer of gases surrounding some planets and stars.

aurora Lights created when *solar wind* gets trapped near Earth's North or South pole.

Big Bang theory A theory that the universe began with a huge explosion.

comet A lump of dirty ice mixed with dust and grit which travels around the *Sun* in an enormous oval-shaped orbit.

constellation A group of *stars* that form a recognizable pattern. There are 88 constellations.

corona The outer layer of the *Sun*.

cosmos Everything in space. Another name for the *universe*.

eclipse The total or partial blocking of one object in space by another. For example, when the **Moon** passes in front of the *Sun*, the *Sun* is eclipsed. This is known as a solar eclipse.

galaxy A huge group of *stars*. There are millions of galaxies in the *universe*.

gas giant A *planet* made up mostly of gas and liquid. Four of the planets in our *Solar System* – Jupiter, Saturn, Uranus and Neptune – are gas giants.

gravity The force of attraction between two objects. The bigger and heavier an object is, the greater its force of attraction.

Kuiper Belt A band of icy rocks that orbit the *Sun* between Pluto and the *Oort Cloud* at the edge of the *Solar System*.

light year The distance that light travels in one year, which is 9.46 million million km (5.88 million million miles).

meteor A *meteoroid* that enters Earth's *atmosphere*. As it passes through the atmosphere, it burns up, making a streak of light. Also known as a *shooting star*.

meteorite A *meteor* that hits the Earth's surface.

meteoroid A small piece of dust or rock that orbits the *Sun*.

meteor shower Lots of meteors, around 20 to 50 per hour, at regular intervals. This is caused by the Earth moving through a stream of dust left by a *comet*.

Milky Way galaxy The *galaxy* that contains our *Solar System*.

moon A natural *satellite* that orbits a *planet*.

NASA The National Aeronautics and Space Administration, which organizes space exploration on behalf of the United States government. NASA projects include the Space Shuttle missions.

nebula A huge cloud of gas and dust where new *stars* can form.

Oort Cloud A band of *comets* that orbit the *Sun* at the edge of the *Solar System*.

orbit The path of an object as it travels around another. For example, the *planets* orbit the *Sun*.

planet A large object that orbits a *star*. There are nine planets in our *Solar System*.

protostar A cloud of condensed gas and dust, drawn together by *gravity*,

that will eventually form a new *star*.

red giant A type of *star* that has a relatively low temperature and is many times bigger than our Sun.

reusable launch vehicle A type of **spacecraft** that can travel to space and back again and again.

rover A small robotic vehicle that travels over the surface of a *planet* or *moon* collecting information and taking photographs.

satellite Any object that orbits another object. *Moons* are natural satellites. Artificial satellites are machines that are launched into space.

shooting star Another name for a *meteor*.

solar flare A sudden burst of energy from a small part of the *Sun's* surface.

solar system A *star* and everything in *orbit* **around** it. Our Solar System includes the *Sun* and all the objects that orbit it, including the

Earth and the Moon.

solar wind A constant stream of invisible gas blown out into space from the *Sun's* surface.

space probe An unmanned spacecraft that collects information about objects in space, such as *planets*.

space station A large, manned spacecraft used as a laboratory and a base for space exploration over a long period of time.

star A huge ball of burning and exploding gas that burns for millions of years, giving off light and heat.

Sun A medium-sized *star* that lies in the middle of our *Solar System*.

sunspot A dark patch that appear on the *Sun's* surface.

universe Everything that exists in space, including *galaxies*, *stars* and *planets*.

white dwarf A small, old *star* that gives off a dim, white light.

Using the Internet ....

Most of the Web sites listed in this book can be accessed with a standard home computer and a Web browser (the software that enables you to display information from the Internet).
We recommend:

- A PC with Microsoft® Windows® 98 or later version, or a Macintosh computer with System 9.0 or later, and 64Mb RAM
- A browser such as Microsoft® Internet Explorer 5, or Netscape® Navigator 4.7, or later versions
- Connection to the Internet via a modem (preferably 56Kbps) or a faster digital or cable line
- An account with an Internet Service Provider (ISP)
- A sound card to hear sound files

Extras

Some Web sites need additional programs, called plug-ins, to play sounds, or to show videos, animations or 3-D images. If you go to a site and you do not have the necessary plug-in, a message saying so will come up on the screen. There is usually a button on the site that you can click on to download the plug-in. Alternatively, go to **www.usborne-quicklinks.com** and click on **Net Help**. Here you can find links to download plug-ins. Here is a list of plug-ins you might need:

RealPlayer® – lets you play video and hear sound files.
Quicktime – enables you to view video clips.
Shockwave® – lets you play animations and interactive programs.
Flash™ – lets you play animations.

Help

For general help and advice on using the Internet, go to **Usborne Quicklinks** at **www.usborne-quicklinks.com** and click on **Net Help**. To find out more about how to use your Web browser, click on **Help** at the top of the browser, and then choose **Contents and Index**. You'll find a huge searchable dictionary containing tips on how to find your way around the Internet easily.

Internet safety

Remember to follow the Internet safety guidelines at the front of this book. For more safety information, go to **Usborne Quicklinks** and click on **Net Help**.

Computer viruses

A computer virus is a program that can seriously damage your computer. A virus can get into your computer when you download programs from the Internet, or in an attachment (an extra file) that arrives with an e-mail. We strongly recommend that you buy anti-virus software to protect your computer and that you update the software regularly.

> ### Internet links
> Go to **www.usborne-quicklinks.com** and type in the keywords "discovery space" for a link to a Web site where you can find out more about computer viruses.

Macintosh and QuickTime are trademarks of Apple Computer, Inc., registered in the U.S. and other countries.
RealPlayer is a trademark of RealNetworks, Inc., registered in the U.S. and other countries.
Flash and Shockwave are trademarks of Macromedia, Inc., registered in the U.S. and other countries.

Index ....

Acknowledgements

Every effort has been made to trace the copyright holders of the material in this book. If any rights have been omitted, the publishers offer to rectify this in any subsequent editions following notification. The publishers are grateful to the following organizations and individuals for their permission to reproduce material (t=top, m=middle, b=bottom, l=left, r=right):

Cover © Digital Vision; **p1** NASA/Science Photo Library; **p2-3** NASA; **p4** © Allan Morton/Dennis Milon/Science Photo Library; **p5** © Victor Habbick Visions/Science Photo Library; **p8l** © Simon Fraser/Science Photo Library; **p8-9b** © Roger Ressmeyer/CORBIS; **p9tr** NASA/ESA; **p9br** NASA; **p10 Sun** Courtesy of SOHO/EIT consortium. SOHO is a project of international cooperation between ESA and NASA; **p10 Venus** Courtesy of NASA/JPL/Caltech; **p10 Earth, Mars** © Digital Vision; **p11 Jupiter, Uranus, Neptune** © Digital Vision; **p11 Saturn** Courtesy of NASA/JPL/Caltech; **p12t** © Professor Jay Pasachoff/Science Photo Library; **p13t** © Chris Madeley/Science Photo Library; **p13b** ESA/Science Photo Library; **p14b, t** NASA; **p15l** © Roger Ressmeyer/CORBIS; **p16l** © Bettmann/CORBIS; **p16r** NASA; **p17l** © Digital Vision; **p17r** NASA; **p18l, tr** NASA; **p18br** NASA/Science Photo Library; **p19t** NASA; **p19b** © Roger Ressmeyer/CORBIS; **p20l, tr, br** © Digital Vision; **p21r** © Digital Vision; **p22l** © David A. Hardy/Science Photo Library; **p23tl** © Digital Vision; **p23b** NASA; **p23r** Courtesy of NASA/JPL/Caltech; **p24-25t** NASA; **p24tl** © Digital Vision; **p24bl** Courtesy of NASA/JPL/Caltech; **p24br** NASA/Science Photo Library; **p25b** NASA; **p26l** NASA/Science Photo Library; **p26 Io, Europa, Ganymede, Callisto** NASA; **p26tr** © Digital Vision; **p27r** Don Davis, NASA/Science Photo Library; **p27tl** © Digital Vision; **p27bl** NASA; **p28tl Uranus** NASA; **p28 Sun, Earth** © Digital Vision; **p28r** © CORBIS; **p28bl** © Digital Vision; **p29t** Courtesy of NASA/JPL/Caltech; **p29tr** © Digital Vision; **p29br Sun, Earth, Neptune** © Digital Vision; **p30l** © Dr. Seth Shostak/Science Photo Library; **p31t** © Rev. Ronald Royer/Science Photo Library; **p32l** © Anglo-Australian Observatory. Photograph by David Malin; **p33t** Digital Vision; **p33bl** Hubble Heritage Team (NASA/AURA/STScI); **p34l** NASA; **p35t** © Digital Vision; **p35bl** NASA Goddard Space Flight Center and the COBE Science Working Group; **p36-37b** © Digital Vision; **p38tl** © Roger Ressmeyer/CORBIS; **p38tr** © Roger Ressmeyer/CORBIS; **p38b** © Digital vision; **p39t, bl** © Digital vision; **p39br** © Dennis di Cicco/CORBIS; **p40l** © Lester V. Bergman/ CORBIS; **p41l, r** NASA; **p42t** © Digital Vision; **p42b** © AFP Photo/Alexander Nemenov; **p43** NASA; **All fact boxes (l)** © Digital Vision.